The Clock Tower Pumpkin

A whimsical tribute to the

MOST EPIC college prank of ALL TIME

Written by
Wendy Larson

Illustrations by
Julia Gash

For Ryan.

I love you, babe, but Cornell is way more beautiful than UCLA

Lean in my friends, *I've a story for you*

It's simple and **fun**, and most of all, true.

It's a tale of **mystery, mystique** and **intrigue**

And it's from the **best school** in the Ivy League.

'Twas a morning like others in the **Ithaca fall**

Beebe Lake flaunted the **foliage** for all

Waterfalls roared 'neath pedestrians' feet

And the crisp, clean air made the setting complete.

Up through Ho Plaza from Willard Straight Hall

Standing an impressive **15 stories tall**

Above Libe Slope, to tell of the hour

Was the **regal** and **stately iconic clock tower.**

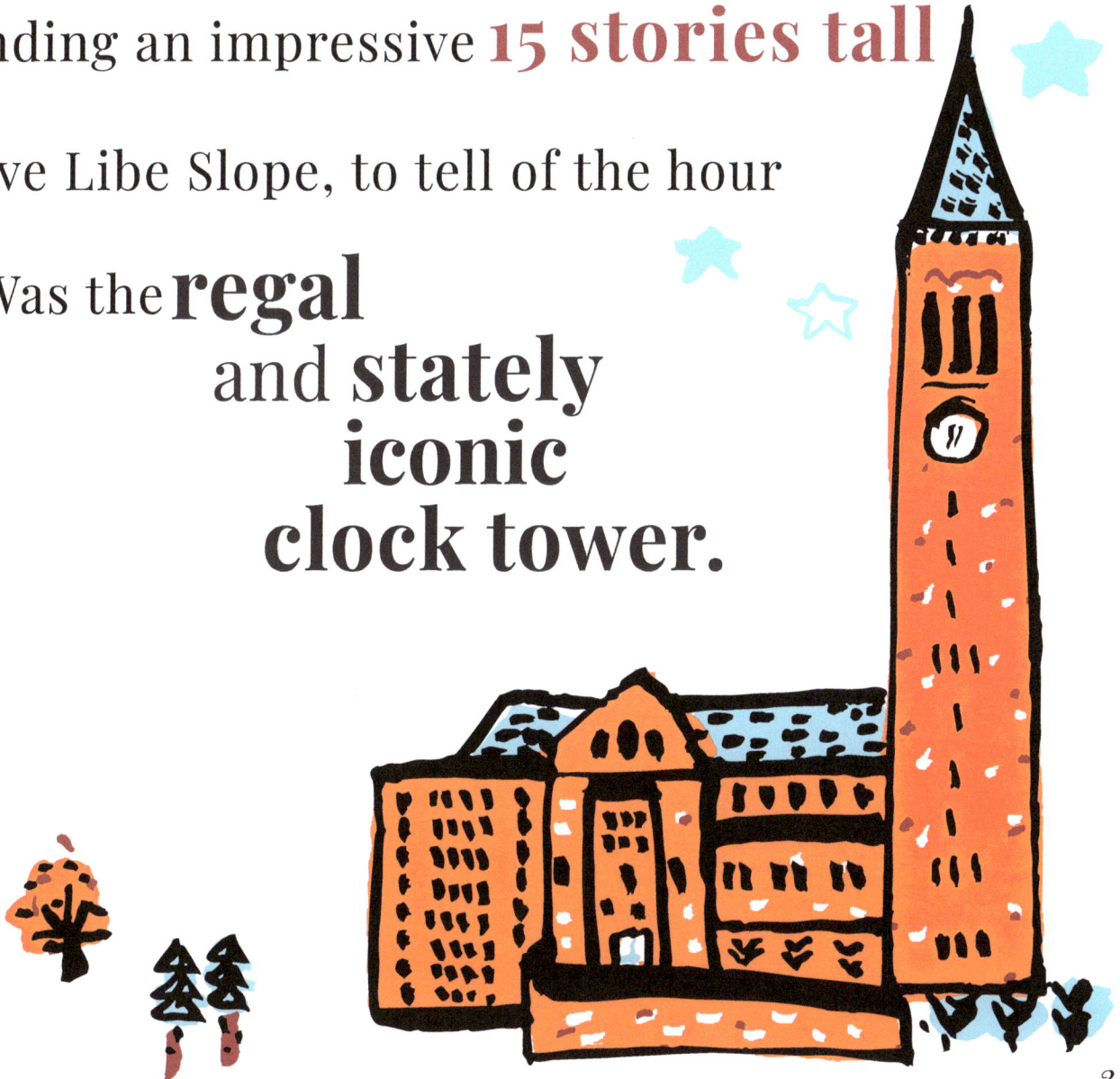

3

Guests would **ascend** the **near-200 stairs**

For *picturesque scenes* with views unimpaired.

Where chimesmasters *played* from a **perch panoramic**

Their songs heard **as far as** the falls of Taughannock.

That day a Cornellian looked up from the quad
Startled to see a phenomenon odd.

On top of the tower was a **sight to admire:**

A 60 pound **pumpkin** impaled on the spire!

What in gourd's name was it doing up there?

And how was it **hoisted** so **high** in the **air?**

Big Red was abuzz at the uncommon sight

And *rumors* soon set the whole campus alight.

Was it really a pumpkin? Some were not sure.

It made the *agenda* on the **campus tour**.

The winter arrived and **who did it**, none guessed,

And the *secretive pranksters* refused to confess.

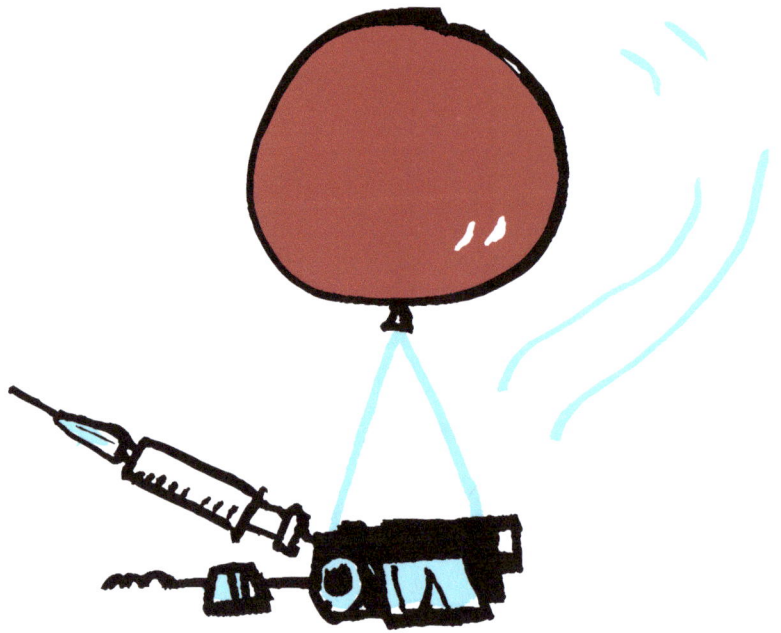

A balloon was dispatched for sample-collecting

With a robot, a camera, and needle for injecting.

The results were returned, and the verdict was in:

The mysterious mass was indeed a **pumpkin.**

The ag school kids worked on quick calculations

To bet on the **length** of the **pumpkin's** duration.

With the chilliest of *winds* and **confounders** at **play**

They **projected** the most likely rate of decay.

The Daily Sun detailed with **regular reports**

Citing stats like it did for **Cornell's D-1 sports.**

And to check every day if the **pumpkin** survived

A webcam was mounted to *watch it all live*.

When the snow started ***melting***, that lump still held on,

Growing steadily *softer* with each **springtime dawn**.

And assessing the ***slope of the roof*** with the wall,

Cornell's counsel considered
the risk of a *fall.*

WARNING

FALLING PUMPKIN ZONE

So they sent up a bucket at the end of a crane

On Friday the thirteenth,
a day preordained.

The **botanical fruit** was KNOCKED
down
from
its post

And was *carefully collected*
by the college provost.

Then after a moment of mourning by all,

They sent the **squished squash** off to Uris Hall,

Where the freeze-dried pulp of the **pumpkin's** remains

Was displayed in a jar with the collection of **brains**.

Now ensuring the *fantastical* **tale persists,**

The saga lives on in *fine campus store gifts*.

Plus, the *dairy bar* works with its seasonal team

To offer up **Clock Tower** **Pumpkin** ice cream.

Never will such a **fine** feat be repeated

With the **prank** *of all* **pranks** positively completed.

Surely a record for now and always,

That **pumpkin** had stuck

for **five months**

and **six days.**

And because there is still not a one to **admit it**

We still **do not know** who went up there and **did it.**

So the gifter's glory
remains yet
unclaimed

And the **marvelous mystery**
is left
unexplained.

So along with the **best** of **Big Red** memories,

Is that now-*famous* **pumpkin** preserved by a *freeze*.

We honor the **squash** that held fast to its stake,

Far above the waters of Cayuga Lake.

REFERENCES

Anbinder, Mark H. "Cornell staffer revives 'PumpkinCam' site, twenty years later." *14850.com,* 13 Oct. 2017, https://www.14850.com/10134978-cornell-pumpkin/.

Cornell University Library. *Facebook,* 31 Oct. 2022, https://www.facebook.com/story.php?story_fbid=10159038057654212&id=46044749211.

Croyle, Johnathan. "Throwback Thursday: Cornell pumpkin prank remains mystery after 20 years." *Syracuse.com,* 16 Nov. 2017, https://www.syracuse.com/vintage/2017/11/throwback_thursday_cornell_pumpkin_prank_celebrates_20th_anniversary.html.

Friedlander, Blaine. "Cornell releases Kingsbury commission finding: 'It is a pumpkin!'" *Cornell Chronicle,* Cornell University, 2 Apr. 1998, https://news.cornell.edu/stories/1998/04/kingsbury-commission-finding-it-pumpkin.

---."Pumpkin prank perpetrator puzzle persists 20 years later." *Cornell Chronicle,* Cornell University, 4 Oct. 2017, https://news.cornell.edu/stories/2017/10/pumpkin-prank-perptrator-puzzle-persists-20-years -later.

Giaimo, Cara. "More than 20 Years Later, Cornell's Great Pumpkin Mystery Remains Unsolved." *Atlas Obscura*, 11 Oct. 2017, https://www.atlasobscura.com/articles/cornell-pumpkin-prank-20th-anniversary-mystery.

Manjoo, Farhad. "How The Pumpkin Got on the Tower." *The Cornell Daily Sun*, n.d., https://cornelldailysun.github.io/pumpkin-feature/.

McFadden, Robert D. "A Pumpkin and Hoopla at Cornell Go Splat." *The New York Times,* 14 Mar. 1998, https://www.nytimes.com/1998/03/14/nyregion/a-pumkin-and-hoopla-at-cornell-go-splat.html.

"Welcome to the Pumpkin Watch (PumpkinCam) Redux!" *Cornell University Library*, n.d., http://pumpkin.library.cornell.edu/.

About the Author

Wendy Larson graduated from Cornell University in 2000 (Go Big Red!), where she spent her sophomore year in the shadow of the clock tower pumpkin. She is an award-winning trademark lawyer by day (and some nights and weekends), an author in her spare time, and a wife and mom always.

About the Illustrator

Julia Gash is the founder and director of Julia Gash Enterprises, a British lifestyle brand, in which she designs whimsical portraits of places around the world. Her best-selling collections are sold in collegiate bookstores, destination retailers, luxury hotels and much-loved museums throughout the world. She lives with her two cats and four chickens, working from her home in the beautiful, coastal town of Dartmouth in Devon.

Julia@juliagash.co.uk   www.linkedin/juliagash

www.juliagash.co.uk

www.ingramcontent.com/pod-product-compliance
Lightning Source LLC
Chambersburg PA
CBHW041547260326
41914CB00016B/1574

*9 7 9 8 2 1 8 6 5 9 7 2 1 *